William Bolcom

Concert Suite

For E♭ Alto Saxophone and Band

E♭ Alto Saxophone and Piano Reduction

<table>
<tr><td>I.</td><td>Lively</td></tr>
<tr><td>II.</td><td>Like an Old Folk Song</td></tr>
<tr><td>III.</td><td>Scherzando</td></tr>
<tr><td>IV.</td><td>Introduction and Jump</td></tr>
</table>

Duration: *ca.* 14 minutes

Commissioned by the University of Michigan Band Alumni
for the 100th Anniversary of the University of Michigan Bands

World Premiere April 9, 1999 at the University of Michigan, Ann Arbor, Michigan.
Written expressly for the University of Michigan Symphony Band and saxophonist Donald Sinta.

Copyright © 1998

EDWARD B. MARKS MUSIC COMPANY / EXCLUSIVELY DISTRIBUTED BY HAL•LEONARD® CORPORATION

7777 W. BLUEMOUND RD. P.O. BOX 13819 MILWAUKEE, WI 53213

PROGRAM NOTE

Concert Suite for E♭ Alto Saxophone and Band (1998) was written specifically for the University of Michigan Symphony Band and the famed professor of saxophone Donald J. Sinta. It was commissioned by the University of Michigan Band Alumni Association and is one in a series of four original works for the band's centennial celebration in 1997.

About the *Concert Suite* Bolcom relates the following:

A major feature of the piece is the extensive use of very high notes – known as "altissimo" – on the alto saxophone. (One might get them easier on a soprano, but that would be cheating!) This is Professor Sinta's specialty and one of the many reasons he is so sought-after as a teacher, and so I felt impelled to throw a few very, very high notes at him that were perhaps over the edge of playability. At first Don swore that many notes were impossible, and I changed one or two, but very soon he called: "Don't change any more notes – I'm taking the challenge!" So the piece is a four-movement high-wire act.

The *Suite* incorporates influences from my composing life. The first movement, *Lively*, is reminiscent of my beloved teacher, Darius Milhaud; the folksong-like second movement incorporates a simple melody that I have heard in my head most of my life. *Scherzando* is a fast triple-time waltz, followed by *Introduction and Jump*, evoking the detective dramas of early television.

William Bolcom

Full score and parts on rental from:
Thedore Presser Company
588 North Gulph Road
King of Prussia, PA 19406

———

INSTRUMENTATION

1st Flute	1st E♭ Alto Saxophone	Baritone Bass Clef
2nd Flute	2nd E♭ Alto Saxophone	Basses (Tubas)
Piccolo	B♭ Tenor Saxophone	String Bass
1st Oboe	E♭ Baritone Saxophone	Timpani
2nd Oboe (English Horn)	E♭ Alto Saxophone Solo	Percussion I (Snare Drum,
E♭ Clarinet	1st Horn in F	Bass Drum, 3 Tom-Toms,
1st B♭ Clarinet	2nd Horn in F	Drumkit)
2nd B♭ Clarinet	3rd Horn in F	Percussion II (Triangle,
3rd B♭ Clarinet	4th Horn in F	3 Graduated Suspended
E♭ Alto Clarinet	1st B♭ Trumpet	Cymbals, Pair of Cymbals,
B♭ Bass Clarinet	2nd B♭ Trumpet	Gong, Wood Block,
B♭ Contrabass Clarinet	3rd B♭ Trumpet	Small Slapstick)
1st Bassoon	1st Trombone	Percussion III (Bells,
2nd Bassoon	2nd Trombone	Crotales, Chimes, Xylophone)
	3rd Trombone	

*Centennial Commission by the University of Michigan
Band Alumni Association*

CONCERT SUITE
for Eb Alto Saxophone and Band

I. Lively

Piano reduction by
Evan Hause

WILLIAM BOLCOM (1998)

NB: In music without key signature,
accidentals obtain only
throughout a beamed group:

 = all Ab

5

CONCERT SUITE

CONCERT SUITE

8

CONCERT SUITE

CONCERT SUITE

II. Like an Old Folksong

CONCERT SUITE

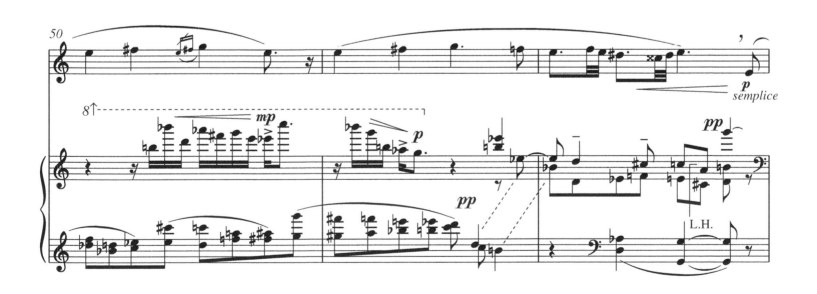

14

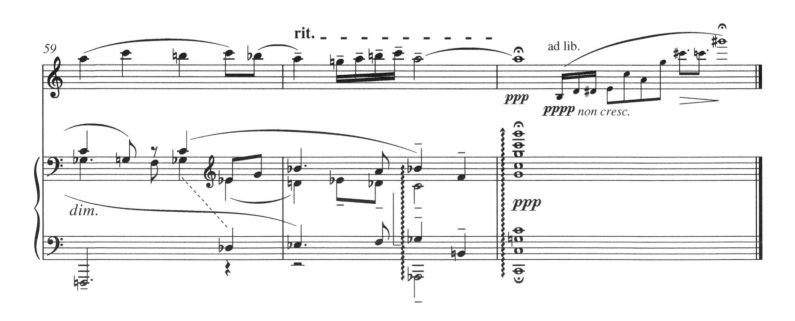

III. Scherzando

Centennial Commission by the University of Michigan
Band Alumni Association

CONCERT SUITE
for E♭ Alto Saxophone and Band

E♭ ALTO SAXOPHONE

WILLIAM BOLCOM (1998)

I. Lively

NB: In music without key signature,
accidentals obtain only
throughout a beamed group: = all A♭

II. Like an Old Folksong

III. Scherzando

V.S.

This page is blank to facilitate upcoming page turn.

IV. Introduction and Jump

10   Concert Suite – E♭ Alto Saxophone

(small notes: *ossia*)

CONCERT SUITE

CONCERT SUITE

20

CONCERT SUITE

IV. Introduction and Jump

22

CONCERT SUITE

23

24

CONCERT SUITE

CONCERT SUITE

CONCERT SUITE

CONCERT SUITE

CONCERT SUITE